The Royal Alphabet A Collection of African Empires in World History

Written by: Maame Serwaa

Published by Melanin Origins LLC
PO Box 122123; Arlington, TX 76012

First Edition

Library of Congress Control Number: 2019936397

ISBN: 978-1-62676-700-3 hardback
ISBN: 978-1-62676-706-5 paperback
ISBN: 978-1-62676-705-8 ebook

I dedicate this book to you, my wonderful readers! Your curiosity and support landed you here and I am beyond grateful and appreciative. I thank you dearly for inspiring creativity in me and I can only hope that I do the same for you as you journey through this book. In all you do, continue to educate yourself with such books that speak of your power and heritage.

So much love,

Maame

How cool is it to know that history began with black history millions of years ago! It is even cooler to know that black history did not start with slavery but rather with Royalty and Riches and Big Empires that thrived for thousands and thousands of years. Learning about the amazing melanin kings and queens that we came from is so refreshing and exciting!

Our history is deep! Our history is rich! Our history is powerful and will always remain important. Join us on this fun and educational journey as we use the alphabets to learn of some great ancient kingdoms in Africa. There were far more than twenty-six rulers and empires of course, but we chose one for every letter in the alphabet to learn about.

Let's explore!

Amina

Queen Aminatu, simply known as Queen Amina, was the first General of the Hausa Army in the Zazzau Kingdom in what is known as Northern Nigeria today. Queen Amina was strong and tough, and fought very hard to expand her kingdom. She had huge walls built around her cities for protection and even today, many of them still stand in remembrance of her.

Behanzin

King Behanzin Hossu Bowelle was known as the King Shark. He was the most influential King in his time who ruled in the powerful West African Dahomey Kingdom. King Behanzin loved his people and his culture very much and always fought off foreigners to keep his people free and happy for as long as he ruled.

Cleopatra

Cleopatra VII is often referred to as the last true pharaoh of Egypt and became goddess at the age of 18. She was known to be beautiful, powerful, intelligent and ambitious. She ruled most of the Middle East and her influence stretched as far as Europe. Egypt became wealthier and flourished under Cleopatra and even after her rule.

Dohemian Female Army

Dohomey was a wealthy empire in West Africa known for its trade and army. With these brave women fighting and protecting the King, Dohomey continued to remain strong and successful.

Ezana of Aksum

Ezana of Aksum (Eritrea today), was known to always have concern for his people and did all he can to grant their wishes. Because of this he was loved very much by the public who were also pleased with decisions for Aksum.

Fasilides

Fasilides was an Emperor of Ethiopia who is credited with founding a city called Gondar that he made Ethiopia's capital at that time.

Ghana Empire

The Ghana Empire was the first of the great trading empires of western Africa in the 7th century. With salt, gold, and ivory trading, the empire grew wealthy and popular. Today, Mali and Mauritania are the two countries that are located where the great Ghana Empire used to be.

Hatshepsut

Queen Hatshepsut was one of the few women to become a pharaoh in Egypt. She ruled for twenty years, making her the longest ruling woman pharaoh in history. She was known for starting several projects which brought about amazing buildings that were never before seen. She also sent her people out on a successful voyage to explore the surrounding land called Punt. This Queen was all about creating and advancing.

Ismail of Morocco

Ismail ibn Sharif is known as one of the most important rulers in Moroccan history. Even though he was very strict, he was also well respected for keeping Morocco free from European rule. His large army fought several European countries to free their cities from colonization.

Jolof Empire

After the decline of the Ghana Empire came the rise of the Jolof Empire. This Empire was made up of the Wolof people who are the largest ethnic group in Senegal and parts of Gambia today. They thrived from trade and although the empire later broke apart into smaller kingdoms, Jolof remained the dominant one.

Kaabu Empire

The Kaabu Empire was a Mandinka kingdom of Senegal and Gambia (Senegambia). The Mandinka is one of the largest ethnic groups in West Africa. Kaabu was initially part of the Mali Empire but became a big independent kingdom of its own when the Mali Empire declined.

Luba Empire

The Luba Empire was made up of several states in Central Africa, which is present-day Congo. Although the people of this Empire were of different origins and backgrounds, they spoke languages that were closely related and shared many similar cultural practices. This makes them a unique group of people in African history.

Mansa Musa

The great Mansa Musa of the Mali Empire is thought to be the richest person to have ever lived and it is even more amazing that he remains the richest person even today. He owned too much gold to count or measure. His horses were even dressed in gold and sprinkled gold on the ground as he traveled. He was brilliant, kind and very generous. Mansa means King of Kings or Emperor and every King who ruled in the Mali Empire received that title.

Nefertiti

Nefertiti was a Queen and the wife of Pharaoh Akhenaten. Her name means "a beautiful woman has come," which supports the many descriptions of how beautiful she was. Her and her husband worked as a team to bring many changes and improvements to Egypt during their reign.

Osei Tutu I

Nana (King) Osei Tutu is best known as the founder and first king of the Ashanti kingdom of modern day Ghana. He successfully united all the Asante states including their Kings, to be under one kingdom. His title then became Asantehene (king of all Asante). With the support of his chief priest, Anokye, Osei Tutu ruled the Ashanti kingdom for nearly twenty years until his death.

Piye

Piye, also known as the first black pharaoh, was a Nubian king out of Kush (Sudan). He was so successful in ruling and expanding his kingdom that he ruled nearly all of Egypt at one point during his time. The black pharaohs were referred to as such because of the beautiful, unique, dark skin tones the Nubians possessed. This dark complexion was respected and valued as a sign of power.

Queen of Sheba

Makeda, better known as Queen of Sheba is one of the most popular figures in ancient history. She is referred to as Queen of the Ethiopian nations. She was very wealthy, smart, influential, and possessed a beauty that has been talked about for centuries.

Ranavalona III

Queen Ranavalona III is best known as the last Queen of Madagascar. On her twenty second birthday, she inherited the throne from her aunt, Ranavalona II. Queen Ranavalona III continuously resisted colonization from the French during her reign by making any necessary changes and never gave up fighting for Madagascar until she was eventually exiled to Algeria.

Sundiata Keita

Although the son of a king who proclaimed Sundiata was destined for greatness, he was treated poorly due to his disability of being crippled. Regardless of losing his family at a young age he grew healthy and brave, overcoming his disability and creating the great Mali Empire. This empire thrived for three hundred years, with Sundiata being its very first Mansa (King of Kings). Because Sundiata's last name means lion, he is often referred to as "Mansa Sundiata Keita, the Lion King of Mali". His grandnephew was Mansa Musa.

Tenkamenin

The people's king is how King Tenkamenin was referred. He was well loved by the people of Ghana and even though his reign was short, Ghana reached its highest success and riches while King Tenkamenin was in power. He is most famous for taking his time each day to listen to people's concerns and always trying to grant their wishes and needs.

Ugandan empire

The beginnings of the powerful Ugandan Kingdom began with Buganda, named after the Ganda people. The Gandas emerged from a small group to becoming a big influential Empire in East Africa. The Empire expanded and prospered for years until foreign influences blended into its political system, leading to a decline of the Kingdom.

Vamwene

A long line of queens ruled in the Mbandu kingdom in modern day Angola. They were all named Vamwene, after the very first Queen, Vamwene Naama. It is astonishing to know that these queens ruled successfully during a time when there were so many controversies surrounding women rulers.

Wattasid Dynasty

The Wattasid Dynasty was a ruling Dynasty in Northern Morocco. Although politics, colonization, and the economy slowed its growth during the height of this Dynasty, it sustained a long rule and persevered. A new Dynasty which developed out of the South successfully helped keep the country from Portuguese colonization.

Xhosa Empire

The Xhosa people are one of the oldest and largest groups in South Africa. Through many changes and attempts by Europeans to colonize them, they fought for over one hundred years to preserve their language and culture, and to keep their independence.

Yaa Asantewaa

During the British attempt to colonize West Africa, many Kingdoms and Empires had to come together and fight them off. In Ghana, Queen Mother Nana Yaa Asantewaa was the single most important voice that encouraged the people of the Ashanti Kingdom not to give up. When all the chiefs were afraid to continue fighting, Yaa Asantewaa gave a powerful speech that inspired the people to persevere. She is known in history to be the last woman to have led a major war against colonizers.

Zulu kingdom

The Zulu kingdom was a small group of people in South Africa until its young leader, Shaka rose to power. With the help of his mother, whom he appointed as queen and his advisor, Shaka Zulu expanded the kingdom and made Zululand a dominant group in South Africa. Today, the Zulu people are the largest group in the country, surviving many wars and phases of colonization, including the apartheid.